Trends in HIP-HOP Dance

DANCE & FITNESS TRENDS

Marylou
Morano
Kjelle

Mitchell Lane
PUBLISHERS
P.O. Box 196
Hockessin, DE 19707

African Dance Trends
Get Fit with Video Workouts
Line Dances Around the World
Trends in Hip-Hop Dance
Trends in Martial Arts
The World of CrossFit
Yoga Fitness
Zumba Fitness

Printing
1   2   3   4   5   6   7   8   9

Library of Congress
Cataloging-in-Publication Data

Kjelle, Marylou Morano.
 Trends in hip-hop dance / by Marylou Morano Kjelle.
    pages cm. — (Dance and fitness trends)
 Includes bibliographical references and index.
 ISBN 978-1-61228-555-9 (library bound)
 1. Hip-hop dance—Juvenile literature. I. Title.
 GV1796.H57K54 2015
 793.3—dc23
                                                    2014006932

eBook ISBN: 9781612285955

PBP

Contents

Introduction..4

Chapter One

"B-Boys, Are You Ready? B-Girls, Are You Ready?"..........7

Disco, Meet Hip-Hop 11

Chapter Two

"To the Beat, Y'all" 13

Ready to Learn? Hip-Hop to It! 19

Chapter Three

Give Me a Break!—Old School Hip-Hop Dance.............. 21

Hip-Hop Roots: Historical Notes 27

Chapter Four

Breaking Through: Hip-Hop Dance in the Mainstream..... 29

Crazy for Hip-Hop Dance 35

Chapter Five

Hip-Hop's New World 37

So . . . You Want to Be a Hip-Hop Dancer? 41

Where to Get Started 42

Timeline 43

Further Reading... 44

Books 44

On the Internet.. 44

Works Consulted 44

Glossary 46

Index... 47

Staying healthy and fit has never been more important. And with hip-hop dance, it has never been more fun. Most young people enjoy listening to popular music and practicing cool dance moves; using them in a hip-hop dance fitness program is a great way to get in shape.

There are many benefits to using hip-hop dance as a workout routine. Hip-hop dance uses the body's strongest muscles, including those of the arms and legs. Working these muscles tones and strengthens them, makes you strong and lean, and gives you endurance. Hip-hop moves support your cardiopulmonary system, giving you a healthy heart and lungs. Hip-hop dancing also burns calories. It's great at relieving stress, and as you become a better hip-hop dancer,

Introduction

your overall self-confidence will increase as well. All of these factors make hip-hop dance a great workout routine for both kids and adults.

Hip-hop dance is becoming such a popular way to exercise that many schools are offering after-school hip-hop dance classes as a way to get kids moving. In addition, hip-hop dance gives kids and teens a positive and creative way to express themselves.

With so many benefits, why not give it a try? Hip-hop dance is a great way to spend time with friends, meet new people, and above all, keep fit. You'll be having so much fun that you'll forget you're also doing something good for your body!

DJ Kool Herc announces the launch of "Hip-Hop Won't Stop: The Beat, The Rhymes, The Life," the first ever hip-hop initiative at the Smithsonian's National Museum of American History in New York, on February 28, 2006. The multi-year project is tracing hip-hop from its origins in the 1970s to its status today.

Chapter 1

"B-Boys, Are You Ready?
B-Girls, Are You Ready?"

Take a hot, summer night, a bunch of inner-city kids with nothing to do, and a teenaged DJ (disc jockey) from Jamaica with a powerful sound system. Bring them all together and what do you have? A new cultural phenomenon called hip-hop.

The year was 1973. The kids were mainly African American and Latino teens hanging out in the parks and on the streets of the Bronx, a section of New York City. And the DJ was Kool Herc, the father of hip-hop.

Herc, whose given name is Clive Campbell, came to the United States in 1967. His friends called him "Hercules" because he was a big guy who was good in sports. Later he shortened the nickname to "Herc." Music was an important part of Herc's life as he was growing up. His father, Keith Campbell, was an auto mechanic and the soundman for a band. Herc went on gigs with them and entertained the audience by playing records when the band took its breaks. Sometimes he spun records the way it was done in Jamaica, by "toasting," or talking over the music as it played.

By the time the summer of 1973 rolled around, Herc had been DJing for a few years. He organized and promoted his own dance parties, often renting the recreation room of the housing project at 1520 Sedgwick Avenue, where he lived with his family. To meet his expenses, Herc charged an admission fee of twenty-five cents for girls and fifty cents for boys. He always packed the house, mainly because of his unusual record collection. When you went to a party hosted by DJ Kool Herc, you knew you'd hear songs that weren't on the radio.

Herc liked to watch the crowd as he spun the vinyl, and as he did, he noticed something. The partygoers often waited for the part of the song with a loud, steady percussion, or drum beat, before getting up to dance. During these segments of a record, the rhythm was pure instrumental with a strong beat; there were no lyrics. Herc called these segments "breaks" or "break beats." During the breaks the dancers would "get down" and show off their wildest dance moves. They dropped to the floor, and then quickly rose to the beat. At other times they balanced on their hands, which left their legs free to move. Sometimes a few of the guys would stage competitions on the dance floor and try to out-do each other with crazy-mad moves they made up right on the spot. But the breaks, which lasted just a few seconds, were never long enough for the dancers to show off all their fancy footwork.

Herc figured he could lengthen the percussion breaks with two turntables, a mixer, an amp and two speakers, which he called the Herculords. Jamming with two turntables wasn't a new idea. It even had a name; DJs called it "turntabling," and they used it to change records or "cut" smoothly from the end of one song to the beginning of the next. Herc's idea was a little different. He played two copies of the same record, one on each turntable, at the same time. He cut back and forth between the two records by lifting the turntables' needles and dropping them back on the vinyl. This allowed him to replay the same part of the record over and over again, which lengthened the break from several seconds to several minutes. He could also play the breaks of different records together. Herc called this going back and forth the "merry-go-round." It gave the dancers exactly what they wanted: more time to dance.

Many years later, Herc looked back on those early days of hip-hop dancing and explained why he created the merry-go-round. "I started playing [music] from a dancefloor perspective.

Turntabling Turntabling

I always kept up the attitude that I'm not playing it for myself, I'm playing for the people out there," he said.

The crowd loved dancing to the break beats. Soon Herc was skipping most of the song and focusing only on the breaks. ". . . [O]nce they heard that, that was it, wasn't no turning back. They always wanted to hear breaks after breaks after breaks after breaks," said Herc. This repetitious beat, which sounded a lot like the music of the Caribbean, was the starting point of hip-hop music and dance.

Herc called the dancing done during the break beats, "break dances." The dancers who danced during the breaks he called "b-boys" and "b-girls." "B-boys, are you ready? B-girls, are you ready?" he would shout into the crowd as he was preparing to cut to a break in a record.

Herc was the most popular DJ in the Bronx in the early 1970s. When his parties got too large for recreation rooms, he moved them to parks, and then to clubs in the Bronx, like the Hevalo, which could pack in several hundred people. Soon his new sound, and the dancing that it gave rise to, reached other parts of New York City. Within a few years, people throughout the United States and the whole world knew of Herc's new hip-hop music and dancing.

B-boying was an early expression of the hip-hop culture. It gave kids and young adults a way to compete without violence.

But that was all still to come. No one suspected on those hot, summer nights in 1973 that breaks and break dancing were the beginning of a new movement called "hip-hop." Nor did anyone realize that a new style of playing and dancing to music would grow into a way for young people to stand up and be noticed. It's been more than forty years since DJ Kool Herc and his music brought about hip-hop dancing, and the world hasn't been the same since.

Not bad for a guy who wasn't even twenty years old!

Disco, Meet Hip-Hop

DJing and b-boying continued to grow in popularity in the Bronx and Harlem. But the rest of the world, immersed in the disco music of the '70s, was clueless about the new hip-hop music and dance coming out of New York City. This changed in 1979, when The Sugarhill Gang released "Rapper's Delight." The fourteen-minute recording used the beat from "Good Times," a number-one recording by Chic, one of disco's most popular groups. But instead of singing the song's original lyrics, the members of The Sugarhill Gang, a three-man group, each took a turn rapping over the music. "Rapper's Delight" was not the first rap single to be released, but it was the first to successfully reach a worldwide audience. It sold millions of copies, reached number four on the Billboard Hot Soul Singles and number thirty-six on the Hot 100 chart. "Rapper's Delight" was important for another reason as well. It marked the beginning of a musical era in which lyrics no longer depended on melody to communicate a message. The glitz and glitter of disco was beginning to be replaced by the music of the streets.

DJ Kool Herc and Grandmaster Flash are two of hip-hop's pioneers. Their new ways of presenting music grew into an entirely new way of life.

Chapter 2
"To the Beat, Y'all"

The hip-hop culture, or lifestyle, began to emerge in the 1970s in the ghettos of the Bronx, a borough of New York City. Several events brought hip-hop about. The 1960s and '70s were turbulent decades for the United States. The civil rights movement, the Vietnam War, the resignation of President Richard M. Nixon, and the women's movement all occurred during these years. On the local level, many state-sponsored programs that benefitted poorer communities were phased out. Society was in turmoil as the American people reacted to the many changes caused by these events. All across America, young people began to realize that they too had a voice. They were speaking up and letting others know how they felt about the things that mattered to them.

The South Bronx in the 1970s was a stretch of neglected buildings and abandoned lots where apartments once had stood. People referred to this area as a war zone because it looked as though a bomb had fallen on the neighborhood. In a way, this was an accurate description. Those living in the South Bronx waged war against poverty, gang activities, drugs, and violence every day.

This is the place where hip-hop was born. It was created by inner-city youth who needed to break free from a world where the odds were stacked against them. These young people didn't want to be defined by their circumstances; they wanted to rise above them. Hip-hop gave them a way to do this.

The hip-hop culture grew to include four elements. In addition to the DJ and b-boys and b-girls, there was the MC, or master of ceremonies who provided additional entertainment by reciting rhyming verse over the music, and there were graffiti artists. Many people were involved in more than one element. For example, a b-boy might also be a graffiti artist, or a graffiti artist might also be an MC. The one thing that connected all four elements was rhythm. These four foundations of hip-hop came together in the 1970s to create an entirely new way of life, which spread to new ways of acting, thinking, dressing, and talking.

DJ Kool Herc jump-started a whole new lifestyle with b-boying and break beats, but other DJs took the idea and ran with it. One of these people was Kevin Donovan, a.k.a. DJ Afrika Bambaataa. He was the first to call this new youth movement "hip-hop." Inspired by Kool Herc, Bambaataa made music with drum machines and synthesizers. He also believed hip-hop didn't have to be one set type of music. He mixed calypso, reggae, and rock by Pink Floyd or the Rolling Stones in with the break beats. Sometimes he played records that no one had ever heard of. "When you came to an Afrika Bambaataa party, you. . . . knew that you was going to hear some weird type of stuff," Bambaataa himself explained.

As a member of the Black Spades, one of the Bronx's most notorious street gangs, Bambaataa had a mission. He wanted to make positive changes in the poverty-stricken and drug-infested neighborhoods of the South Bronx. Shortly after DJ Kool Herc began cutting his first breaks on vinyl records, Bambaataa formed a group of street kids into a five-member team of break dancers, which he named the Zulu Kings. Bambaataa also formed his own crew of DJs, MCs, and graffiti artists, called the Zulu Nation. The Zulus were into more than just music and dancing. They fought street crime and violence and defined principles of hip-hop culture, like knowledge, justice, peace, and respect. Above all, Bambaataa wanted his parties to be a place of unity. Gang members were welcome, but he didn't tolerate gang activity. When they attended

DJ Afrika Bambaataa was once a member of a gang in the South Bronx. Later, he realized that hip-hop could have a positive influence on a young person's life. He and his Universal Zulu Nation brought hip-hop's positive message of love and unity to the rest of the world.

Bambaataa's parties, gang members had to leave their attitude at the door.

The Zulu Kings made break dancing into what it is today by giving rival gangs a new way to compete. Instead of fighting on the streets, they danced. In the early 1980s, the Zulus were the first to bring the hip-hop culture to Europe.

Joseph Saddler, who uses the name DJ Grandmaster Flash, is another early hip-hop dance scene celebrity who grew up in the South Bronx. As a teenager, Flash pulled apart hair dryers and radios to see how they worked. Because he was interested in electronics, his mother sent him to Samuel Gompers Vocational Technical High School, to become an electronics technician. One of Flash's school assignments was to build an amplifier. He didn't just build an amplifier, though. He designed an entire sound system which he called "peek-a-boo" by building small amplifiers to drive the headphones. When he connected the headphones to the mixers, he could listen to one of the records while he spun the other. This let him hear the music in his ears before the people in the room knew what song was coming next. This advantage let him cut to a record right on a beat. Flash also began "back spinning," or spinning a record backward to where the break begins, as a way to repeat a part of that record. Back spinning let Flash play the breaks of a song back-to-back. Flash formed the Furious Five, a group of five MCs who dressed in outrageous outfits. The Furious Five introduced more complicated voice-overs and choreographed dances to the hip-hop scene.

Grand Wizard Theodore made a contribution to hip-hop dancing by "scratching" records when he was just thirteen years old. He was in his bedroom and playing music way too loud, and his mother demanded he turn it down. Theodore used his finger to stop the record while the needle was in the groove of the record. He noticed that if he spun the record back and forth, he could make the noise produced by the scratching become part of the song's rhythm. "I practiced with it and perfected it and used it with different records, and that's when it became a scratch," he said. "What I did was give it a rhythm; I made a tune out of it, rubbing it for three, four minutes . . . "

When the hip-hop dance scene first emerged, the DJ did it all—hosted the party, chose the music, and spun the records. Later, DJs and MCs teamed up. The DJ, no longer having to interact with the crowd, was free to concentrate on spinning records. Grandmaster Flash remembers it this way: "[My MC] found a way to allow me to do my thing and have the people really, really, rocking . . . "

MCs gave themselves names like Kid Creole, Scorpio, Love Bug Starski, and Kool Moe Dee. When they were jamming, MCs were all about entertainment. But when they walked the streets, they had power and respect.

The MC wrote his or her own material. The words didn't always rhyme, but when they did, it sounded like poetry. Some say the MC is a throwback to the West African *griot*, a historian who orally told stories. In addition, MCs used "call and response," also an African tradition brought to America. In "call and response," the MC yells a statement to the crowd, and the crowd responds by yelling back. An example might be:

MC: Yes, yes, y'all, and you don't stop

THE CROWD: To the beat, y'all, and you don't stop

MCs made the party more exciting because call and response made partygoers feel like they were dancing to a live band. Sometimes several MCs worked with one DJ. Grandmaster Flash's MCs were the first to take turns at the mic, before they became the Furious Five. They called this going "back and forth."

Slowly, the focus of hip-hop dancing moved from the DJ and the music to the MC and the spoken words. As time went on, the MC became a jam's main attraction. The MC gave the hip-hop movement its personality. As rappers, (the word *rap* is slang for "talk") the MCs became the voice of hip-hop.

MCing was hip-hop's verbal expression, and its visual expression was graffiti. Graffiti became popular in Philadelphia in the 1960s and quickly spread to New York City. Rival gangs marked their territory by spray painting buildings and other structures, like trains and subways. Entire train cars were covered—end to end and top to bottom in block letters. Painting graffiti on public buildings or property is illegal, so graffiti artists signed their work with fake names, like Seen, Riff, and Mad 103, to keep their identities secret. These signatures were called tags. Often, but not always, several artists worked together in crews. Each graffiti artist expressed his or her own style using colors, patterns, curves, and letters. Just about every imaginable object was drawn as graffiti.

Graffiti was a way of taking possession and demonstrating ownership of a street corner, a block, or a neighborhood. When a graffiti artist put his or her name on a building, it symbolically became the property of the artist. "Graffiti writing is a way of gaining status in a society where to own property is to have identity," said Hugo Martinez, who organized the first graffiti association. Spray painting over graffiti that someone else had created made a statement. "We defend our territory, whatever space we steal to paint on, we defend it fiercely," said one graffiti artist.

Dress was also part of the hip-hop culture. Early hip-hoppers usually wore baggy pants and extra-large sweaters or sweatshirts that featured a favorite sports team. Sneakers with wide, colorful laces, or boots were standard foot gear, while baseball hats and brimmed Kangol hats were worn on the head. Bomber jackets were winter gear. Both boys and girls rounded out their hip-hop outfits with large, flashy pieces of gold and platinum jewelry. Some young people showed they were part of the hip-hop fashion scene by wearing jeans that had been torn or slashed on purpose. Dress was also used to make a statement. For example, when a DJ or MC wore traditional African clothing, it was a form of respect to the land that his or her ancestors came from. Later, rappers began wearing suits, coats, dress shoes, and hats made by high-end clothing designers.

The hip-hop culture formed by accident. It wasn't started by people looking to make a lot of money or become famous. Those who started the hip-hop movement, and the young people who participated in it, wanted the world to notice them and hear what they had to say. The world did take notice, and in a much bigger way than they could ever have imagined.

Ready to Learn? Hip-Hop to It!

Ready to learn hip-hop dance? Like other fitness activities, hip-hop dance can be done alone. But it is much more fun to work out in a class. Most dance schools will let you observe a class before you sign up, or even try your first class for free. People of different ages—not just kids—are learning hip-hop dance. You may prefer to start in a class where all the students are at the same level. This way you can learn together.

Hip-hop dance is taught as a combination of structure and spontaneity. There's lots of repetition to help you learn the steps. That's the structure. Once you've got those moves down, you'll be able to incorporate your own attitude into your dance. That's the spontaneity. Expect to move to loud music with a heavy beat.

One advantage of hip-hop dance is that you don't have to go to a gym to work out. You do, however, have to have enough space to move. Another advantage is that no special equipment is needed. Comfortable clothes like baggy sweatpants and loose-fitting T-shirts will allow you to move easily. Sneakers or tennis shoes are great for dancing. If you learn complicated moves, like the windmill, you may want to wear knee pads and elbow pads for protection. Be sure to warm up first and don't overexert yourself. And stop dancing right away if you start hurting. With all workouts, it's always best to practice good common sense!

Dance Fitness

Toprocking is dancing done in the upright position. Along with downrocking, power moves, and freezes, toprocking is one of the four basic moves of b-boying. Toprocking allows the dancer to incorporate his or her own style into the dance.

Chapter 3

Give Me a Break!— Old School Hip-Hop Dance

Surf the channels of your TV, and chances are you'll see a hip-hop dance or two in a movie, television show, sporting event, or even in a commercial. But hip-hop dancing wasn't always so in-your-face. In fact, when it began in the 1970s, it was called an underground movement because only a few people knew about it or danced in the hip-hop style. This very early hip-hop is now considered "old school."

Early hip-hop dance consisted of basic moves and styles. One was "toprocking," which was dancing upright. Toprocking had no rules, so b-boys and b-girls freestyled when they toprocked. This means they spontaneously incorporated different dance moves as they went along. Martial arts films may have been an influence on this style of dancing. In Brooklyn, New York, a similar dance style developed called uprocking. Unlike toprocking, uprocking is done with a partner. With its jumps, turns, jerks, and aggressive arm movements, uprocking often resembles hand-to-hand combat.

Another basic element of early b-boying was downrock, or floor work. These were moves that were done on the floor while the hands and arms supported the body. The dancers would also freeze, or hold a position, at any point in the dance. These moves, which emerged around 1974, moved hip-hop dance into its second stage. One classic breaking move is the six-step, where a dancer moves in a circle on the hands. The feet move in and out around the hands which support the body in the middle. Power moves, which require a lot of speed and strength, began to be used during this stage. Head spins and back spins, freezes, and windmills (a back spin with flaring

Uprocking is an aggressive street dance that is done with a partner. Because it consists of forceful and determined arm moves, uprocking sometimes resembles more of a street fight than a street dance.

leg action), are all examples of power moves. By the late 1970s, break dancers had begun to collaborate, practicing and dancing in small groups called crews. Freestyling kept the dances fresh and new and gave them personality.

G.L.O.B.E. and Pow Wow are two rappers who were early break dancers. They explain their moves: ". . . We started kicking side to side and hitting the ground. Jump down, bend, crouch and take a set, all down, doing whatever moves we could, spinning top, sweep, back spin. . . . [Y]ou'd fall, touch your hand on the ground, improvise something, bounce right up, and freeze."

Since a lot of space is needed for a power move, breaking moved to the inside of a cypher—a circle of spectators that formed around the b-boys. Competitions in the cyphers were called battles. The battles gave the dancers, who were often members of gangs, a way to compete without violence or bloodshed. In early battling, the spectators decided the winner, based on the style and complexity of the dancer's moves. Later, more formal competitions were decided by experienced judges. In either competition, winners took away the most valued of prizes: the respect of the community.

Around the same time that New York dancers were defining their breaking style, dancers on the West Coast were creating a style of their own called West Coast funk. Popping and locking are two early hip-hop dances that started during the West Coast funk movement. Popping was created by a dancer from Fresno, California, named Sam Solomon, who went by the name Boogaloo Sam. The dance involves contracting and relaxing the muscles of the legs, arms, neck and torso. In this way, the dancer "pops" his joints one after another. The overall effect is that the body

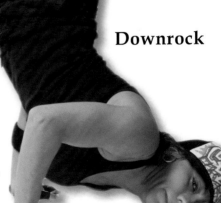

Downrock

The head spin is one of the more popular break dance moves. It is also one of the more difficult. A b-boy named Kid Freeze says he invented this move.

jerks as if a jolt of electricity was running through it. Because of this, New Yorkers called popping "Electric Boogie." The jerky body movements worked well with the percussion beats played during the breaks, and New Yorkers quickly made Electric Boogie part of their street dance scene.

Popping and locking moves are often danced together. When you "pop," you quickly contract and relax the muscles of your arms or legs. When you "lock," you momentarily freeze or "lock" a muscle and then release it. Both popping and locking are playful and comical types of street dancing.

Locking is another West Coast funk dance. It is a variation of popping that was created by Los Angeles dancer Don Campbell. Here, a dancer brings a fast move to a sudden stop, holds the position for a beat or two, then follows the freeze with another fast move. Campbell, who also used the last name, Campbellock, accidentally created locking when he was learning the Funky Chicken dance. Unsure of himself, he would freeze, or "lock up" between dance moves. Although he wasn't trying to be funny, his hesitation made his friends laugh and cheer him on. Realizing he was on to something, Campbell began improvising with freezes. "No matter what type of mistake I made, they clapped," Campbell said. He fell on the floor, but that didn't stop the laughter and cheers. "No matter what I did wrong, I was doing something right!" he explained.

Although two different dance styles emerged from two different parts of the country, eventually both became known as b-boying or break dancing.

As hip-hop became more popular, the style of dance associated with it entered a third phase. B-boying evolved into new energetic and athletic moves like the Running Man and the Roger Rabbit, a dance that combined hopping on alternate legs with pumping of the arms.

Hip-Hop Roots: Historical Notes

Some researchers believe that hip-hop dance can be traced to the African Diaspora, the displacement of Africans that began around the fifteenth century, and to the Middle Passage, the route ships traveled to bring slaves from West Africa to the Americas. Dance scholars believe that three dances that originated around this time are historically related to hip-hop dancing. These dances are known today as the Snake, the Cabbage Patch, and the Running Man. The moves of each dance symbolically tell the story of black oppression and discrimination.

The Snake is a dance that represents survival and the desire to mentally remove oneself from one's surroundings. When dancing the Snake, only the head, neck, and upper torso move; the lower body remains still. The arms are held out to the sides and are slightly bent. Holding this position, the head, neck and shoulders are moved to one side, returned to the center and then moved to the other side.

The Cabbage Patch symbolizes working and achieving, despite seemingly impossible odds. To do this move, the dancer steps in a semi-circle, while the arms swing back and forth.

The Running Man uses the arms, legs, and feet, but the body doesn't move. The feet alternately slide along the floor while running in place. The fists are clenched while the arms pump up and down. The dance symbolizes the anger of working and never getting ahead. The outstretched arms continuously reach for something that is just out of reach and never obtained.

As these dances moved into more modern times, the Snake and the Cabbage Patch were most often performed in the home. The Running Man was usually part of a choreographed performance. Elements of all three dances are seen in modern hip-hop dance.

Washington Wizards guard John Wall does the Dougie onto the basketball court before a game in 2010. Several members of sports teams have performed the dance before, during, and after their games, usually to the fans' delight and the team manager's dismay.

Breaking Through: Hip-Hop Dance in the Mainstream

In the fall of 1980, police were called to the Washington Heights neighborhood of northern Manhattan. A bunch of kids, they were told, were fighting in the subway. When the police arrived, they hauled the kids off to the station. After questioning the youth, the police realized they had made a mistake. The kids hadn't been fighting. They'd been doing "that kind of dancing you do to rapping."

Hip-hop dance has come a long way since the "old school" days of dancing in the streets and in the recreation rooms of housing complexes. As the years passed, new dances were built on older dance moves. Often new and old moves were mixed together to create a new dance. Today's hip-hop dancing has changed significantly, but one thing that remains the same between the old school and new styles of hip-hop dance is that they are danced to a strong beat.

One modern hip-hop dance move is the Dougie. This dance started in Dallas, Texas, and is named for rapper Doug E. Fresh. The dance is based on a series of moves described in the hit song, "Teach Me How To Dougie," by the group Cali Swag District. It's done by stepping from side to side while bending the knees and leaning with the shoulders. The Dougie is a favorite among athletes. In 2010, a clip was posted to YouTube of NBA rookie John Wall doing the Dougie in his warm-up suit before a home debut game with the Washington Wizards. The video went viral. However, there is a time and a place to dance the Dougie. New York Jets wide receiver Braylon Edwards learned this the hard way. He received a

Sean Combs, also known as Diddy, P. Diddy, and Puff Daddy, brought the Harlem Shake to the world in 2001, when his label Bad Boy Records released G. Dep's song "Let's Get It." The video for the song featured kids performing the dance.

penalty for dancing the Dougie after scoring a touchdown against the New England Patriots in September of 2010.

The Harlem Shake is a dance that came out of Harlem in the 1980s. The true way to do the Harlem Shake is to move the shoulders alternately up and down and from front to back. The arms and feet move to the beat of the music. Variations in the shoulder moves and arm waves add personality to the dance. The Harlem Shake has grown in popularity in an odd way. In 2013, a video was posted to YouTube of a group of people in masks and costumes who were satirizing, or making fun of, the original Harlem Shake dance. Shortly after, five teenagers from Queensland, Australia, registered on YouTube as The Sunny Coast Skate, posted an imitation video of the Harlem Shake. As soon as the Australian video was posted, other YouTube users began imitating it and posting their own videos demonstrating their versions of the dance. Within a few days, four thousand imitation Harlem Shake videos were being uploaded to YouTube each day.

Another modern hip-hop dance is the Walk It Out. The dancer squats down slightly and walks

Walk It Out

The dance crew Boxcuttuhz poses for a photograph at the live taping of *America's Best Dance Crew* in Burbank, California, in 2008. Although they lost to Quest Crew, Boxcuttuhz believed they had won the hearts and minds of the American public.

forward, turning the toe, knee, and hip of one side of the body out with each step. The arms and hands can move in a variety of ways. In some respects, the Walk it Out resembles the Twist, a dance made popular in the 1960s by Chubby Checker.

Hip-hop dance has also reinvented itself through television, movies, and the theatre. For seven seasons, MTV broadcasted *America's Best Dance Crew*, a reality show that allowed hip-hop crews to compete for money and the national title. Crews were given a challenge that centered on a specific theme. The contestants had to progress through several rounds before being declared the final winner. The VH1 network has expanded on the hip-hop theme with shows like *I Want to Work for Diddy*. Over three million viewers watched another VH1 hip-hop reality series hit, *T.I. and Tiny: The Family Hustle*, on the first night it aired.

Like television, motion pictures helped hip-hop dance become mainstream. Movies about or including hip-hop dance began appearing in the 1980s. A few of the most popular are *Wild Style*, *Beat Street*, *Breakin'*, and *Krush Groove*. Often, well-known DJs, rappers, and break dancers appeared in these films.

The hip-hop culture has also moved into the computer and video game market. Ubisoft released *The Hip-Hop Dance Experience*, a game for the Wii and Xbox 360 that many people can enjoy at the same time. *B-Boy* was also released for the PlayStation 2 and PSP, where players can build their own breaking crews and battle against celebrity b-boys.

As hip-hop moves into its fifth decade, it is changing with the times. Freestyling is still a part of the dance, but more and more, hip-hop dancing is becoming arranged by trained dancers called choreographers who invent new dances and show other dancers how to do them. This new style of hip-hop dance has made its way into movies, music videos, and television. It is also seen on the stage. Other dance forms, like ballet and jazz, have started to incorporate hip-hop dance moves into their routines.

Freestyling is the process of inventing your own dance on the spot. Let the music be your guide as you string moves together to create your own unique dance.

Some old school hip-hop followers feel that choreographing hip-hop dance has changed it, and even taken away from it. They say that one of the most important things about hip-hop dance is its originality. They remind us that b-boying was built on spontaneous movements of self-expression. They believe that when hip-hop dance is choreographed, it loses its creativity.

Crazy for Hip-Hop Dance

Richard Colon, a.k.a. "Crazy Legs," is one of the people who helped b-boying transition into the modern world. He was just thirteen when he battled for a place in the original Rock Steady Crew and lost, but was accepted anyway. Shortly thereafter, he became the crew's president and took the members to London and France. He starred in hip-hop movies like *Wild Style*, *Style Wars*, and *Beat Street*, sometimes playing himself. In 1991 Crazy Legs appeared in *So! What Happens Now?*, a production that blended rap, dance, and graffiti. A reviewer for *The New York Times* called the show "probably the first hip-hop production on a mainstream dance stage in New York City." Crazy Legs no longer dances, but remains active in hip-hop dance by arranging Rock Steady Crew's anniversary productions and educating youth. Of those early days as a b-boy, Crazy Legs says: "We were just innocently having fun, not realizing that we were setting a foundation for what is a multibillion dollar a year industry."

Crazy Legs (center) and members of the Rock Steady Crew arrive at a party in New York. Crazy Legs, whose real name is Richard Colon, started out as a b-boy in the Bronx. Later, as president of Rock Steady, he brought the team around the world, introducing break dance to many people.

Break dancing is a total body workout. Gradually build up your endurance by starting with easy moves and working your way up to complicated moves like this flare, which requires a lot of upper-body strength.

Chapter 5
Hip-Hop's New World

The hip-hop culture that began on the streets of the Bronx is now enjoyed throughout the world. Part of this expansion is due to cable and satellite television, which allowed MTV to air music videos in Europe, Asia, and elsewhere beginning in 1988.

Each year in Montpellier, France, b-boy and b-girl crews meet for the Battle of the Year (BOTY). To qualify, crews must first compete in local BOTY contests around the world. Once they get to BOTY, crews must then perform a six-minute choreographed routine which is judged on synchronicity, stage presence, theme, music, execution of moves, and the overall performance. The final battles involve unchoreographed, face-to-face contests between individual b-boys or crews. Another organization, Breakin' Convention, stages b-boy events, hip-hop jams, and street dance competitions throughout the United Kingdom.

Nomadic Massive is a multilingual, multicultural hip-hop group based in Montreal. In October 2010, five members of the group traveled to Haiti. Their mission was to conduct a seven-day workshop with young artists who lived in the Carrefour Feuilles neighborhood of Port-au-Prince. This was an area that had been hit hard by the January 2010 earthquake. Nomadic Massive taught writing and performing based on the hip-hop culture. The entertainers helped the young people write and record a song and perform it on television.

Hip-hop dance is here to stay, both in the cyphers of America as well as on European and Asian stages. But there's more to hip-hop than just dancing. People in countries around the world use the hip-hop movement to promote environmental

Members of Dead Prezz crew from Greece perform during the first part of the Battle of the Year Competition in 2010. Each year, BOTY draws break dance crews from around the world to compete to be the b-boy champions of the world. Some people refer to this prestigious event as the "World Cup of B-Boying."

Although it was created in the United States, hip-hop dance is enjoyed throughout the world. Many see the hip-hop culture as a way to unite people, teach tolerance, and increase awareness of social and environmental issues. Here young people in the Asian country of Cambodia learn to break dance in their city of Phnom Penh.

awareness, social justice, and education. From South Africa to Syria to Mexico and all points in between, hip-hop is bringing people together. Regardless of race or ethnicity, hip-hop continues giving a voice to the voiceless, empowering people and teaching tolerance.

So ... You Want to Be a Hip-Hop Dancer?

If you have enjoyed learning about hip-hop culture and dance, you may be interested in a career in this field. There are a number of options for you to consider. You could become a performance dancer, dance instructor, or choreographer. There are formal training programs for those who wish to study hip-hop dance. But not all hip-hop dancers have gone to school to learn their craft. Some learned breaking moves on their own, while others learned from friends who were experienced dancers. Professional dancers star in television shows, music videos, and motion pictures. You may enter competitions both locally and around the world. If you perform on stage, you'll dance before live audiences in a theatre.

Behind-the-scenes positions are available for those who want to work in hip-hop dance, but don't actually want to dance. Some of these positions provide help with lighting, stage sets, and costumes. You could also direct a hip-hop dance production. There are many opportunities to work on incorporating hip-hop dance with technology as well. For example, you could create computer or video games around a hip-hop dance theme.

Colleges and universities throughout the United States offer classes in hip-hop dance, music, writing, and culture. But whether you learn through formal training, by studying videos, or from a friend, education and practice are essential to turning your passion for hip-hop dance into a career of any kind.

Where to Get Started

Many community centers and YMCAs offer hip-hop dance classes. Some private dance studios offer them as well. You can find classes listed under "dance" in the yellow pages of your phone book or online by searching Google for "hip-hop dance instruction" and the city where you live. Prices range from just a few dollars per class to several hundred dollars for a full semester of ten to twelve classes. If there are no classes in your neighborhood, check out your local library to see if you can borrow an instructional hip-hop DVD. You can also find classes online by searching "hip-hop dance instruction." YouTube (youtube.com) has many videos that demonstrate hip-hop dance, and you can view classes and tutorials as well as individual dances.

1920s	Earl "Snakehips" Tucker performs the "Snake Dance" in New York City. Fifty years later, this dance influences break dancing.
1970s	On the West Coast, Don Campbell puts together a series of dance moves which he calls "locking." Locking later becomes part of hip-hop dance.
1972	Young people in the Bronx, New York, dancing to James Brown's hit, "Get on the Good Foot," start improvising wild dance moves during the record's percussion segments.
1973	DJ Kool Herc lengthens the beat of records by using two turntables at parties in the Bronx.
1974	Afrika Bambaataa creates the Zulu Nation.
1975	On the West Coast, "Boogaloo Sam" Solomon creates a series of dance moves which are called "Electric Boogie" on the East Coast; Grand Wizard Theodore creates the "scratch."
1977	Rock Steady Crew is formed.
1978	Grandmaster Flash joins with a group of rappers to form Grandmaster Flash and the Furious Five.
1979	The Sugarhill Gang releases the song, "Rapper's Delight."
early 1980s	The Zulu Nation is the first to bring the hip-hop culture, including hip-hop dance, to Europe.
1982	Grandmaster Flash and the Furious Five release "The Message," the first commercial rap song with political meaning.
1983	The first motion pictures about hip-hop dancing and culture, like *Wild Style* and *Style Wars* are released.
1986	Salt-n-Pepa release their first album, *Hot, Cool & Vicious*, one of the first albums released by a group of all-female rap singers.
1988	MTV creates the show, *Yo! MTV Raps*. It remains on the air until 1995.
2004	The first Breakin' Convention takes place in London.
2010	The group Cali Swag District releases "Teach Me How to Dougie," making the Dougie a popular dance across the country.
2013	Hip-hop music celebrates its fortieth anniversary.
2014	Afrika Bambaataa and other hip-hop pioneers announce plans for the Universal Hip-Hop Museum, scheduled to open in the Bronx in 2017.

Books

Baker, Soren. *The History of Rap and Hip Hop*. Detroit: Lucent Books, 2006.

Fitzgerald, Tamsin. *Hip-Hop and Urban Dance*. Chicago: Heinemann Library, 2009.

Freese, Joan. *Hip-Hop Dancing*. Mankato, MN: Capstone Press, 2008.

Gaines, Ann Graham, and Reggie Majors. *The Hip-Hop Scene: The Stars, The Fans, The Music*. Berkeley Heights, NJ: Enslow Publishers, Inc., 2010.

Hatch, Thomas. *A History of Hip-Hop: The Roots of Rap*. Bloomington, MN: Red Brick Learning, 2006.

Hess, Mickey, ed. *Icons of Hip Hop: An Encyclopedia of the Movement, Music, and Culture*. Westport, CT: Greenwood Press, 2007.

On the Internet

Battle of the Year
    http://www.battleoftheyear.de/
Bboy World
    http://www.bboyworld.com/
The Hip-Hop Dance Conservatory
    http://hdcny.org/
Hip Hop Network
    http://www.hiphop-network.com/
Mahalo.com: Learn Hip Hop Dance
    http://www.mahalo.com/courses/learn-hip-hop-dance/getting-started/
    find-the-beat/

Works Consulted

Banes, Sally. *Writing Dancing in the Age of Postmodernism*. Hanover, NH: Wesleyan University Press, 1994.

Battle of the Year. "About BOTY." http://www.battleoftheyear.de/about.html

Chang, Jeff, ed. *Total Chaos*. New York: Basic Civitas Books, 2006.

Chang, Jeff. *Can't Stop, Won't Stop*. New York: St. Martin's Press, 2005.

Chang, Jeff. "It's a Hip-Hop World." *Foreign Policy*, October 11, 2007. pp. 58–65.

Cobb, William Jelani. *To the Break of Dawn*. New York: New York University Press, 2007.

Cohen, Ben. "What's the Latest Move in Sports? Doing the 'Dougie.' " *The Wall Street Journal*, November 13, 2010. http://online.wsj.com/article/SB10001424052748703805004575606731553244978.html

Dikson. "Hip Hop and Social Change Around the World: An Interview with Nomadic Wax." Matador Network, December 24, 2012. http://matadornetwork.com/change/hip-hop-and-social-change-around-the-world-an-interview-with-nomadic-wax/

Driver, Ian. *A Century of Dance: A Hundred Years of Musical Movement, from Waltz to Hip Hop.* New York: Cooper Square Press, 2000.

Dunning, Jennifer. "Critic's Choice/Daance: Street Dance Moves Up to Mainstream." *The New York Times*, November 22, 1991.

Fricke, Jim, and Charlie Ahearn. *Yes Yes Y'all.* Cambridge, MA: Da Capo Press, 2002.

Gorman, Bill. "Monday Cable Ratings." TV by the Numbers, December 6, 2011. http://tvbythenumbers.zap2it.com/2011/12/06/monday-cable-ratings-chargersjags-down-but-still-tops-pawn-stars-love-hip-hop-closer-rizzoli-isles-wwe-raw-much-more/112771/

Heyden, Tom. "Harlem Shake: Tracking a Meme Over a Month." *BBC News Magazine*, March 1, 2013. http://www.bbc.co.uk/news/magazine-21624109

History.com. "Hip Hop is Born at a Birthday Party in the Bronx." This Day in History. http://www.history.com/this-day-in-history/hip-hop-is-born-at-a-birthday-party-in-the-bronx

Huntington, Carla Stalling. *Hip Hop Dance: Meanings and Messages.* Jefferson, NC: McFarland & Company, Inc., Publishers, 2007.

Light, Alan, ed. *The Vibe History of Hip Hop.* New York: Three Rivers Press, 1999.

Muir, Kristy. "Copycat Shakers Tap into Worldwide Video Hit by Coast Teens." *Sunshine Coast Daily*, February 15, 2013. http://www.sunshinecoastdaily.com.au/news/caloundra-teens-shake-up-net-to-become-video-stars/1756874/

Ogg, Alex, and David Upshal. *The Hip Hop Years: A History of Rap.* New York: Fromm International, 2001.

Perkins, William Eric, ed. *Droppin' Science.* Philadelphia: Temple University Press, 1996.

Stern, Joanna. "'Harlem Shake' Shakes It Across YouTube, With Over 44 Million Views." ABC News, February 13, 2013. http://abcnews.go.com/blogs/technology/2013/02/harlem-shake-shakes-it-across-youtube-with-over-44-million-views/

Westbrook, Alonzo. *Hip Hoptionary: The Dictionary of Hip Hop Terminology.* New York: Harlem Moon Broadway Books, 2002.

Glossary

borough (BUR-oh)—A small, self-governing section of a city.

commercialization (kuh-mur-shuh-lahy-ZAY-shuhn)—Profiting from something.

choreography (kawr-ee-OG-ruh-fee)—The art of creating a dance, arranged in a routine.

debut (dey-BYOO)—The first showing.

endurance (en-DOOR-uhns)—The ability to do something for long periods of time.

ghetto (GET-oh)—A poor, crowded section of a city occupied by minorities.

improvise (IM-pruh-vahyz)—To create without planning or preparing beforehand.

mainstream—The tastes of a large part of, or most of, society.

monetary (MON-ih-ter-ee)—Having to do with money.

notorious (noh-TAWR-ee-uhs)—To be publicly known for a particular reason.

reinvent—To remake in a new or different way.

soundman—A technician who is responsible for a sound system's performance.

synchronicity (sing-kruh-NIHS-ih-tee)—The state in which things or events happening together or at the same time.

torso (TAWR-soh)—The trunk of the human body.

turbulent (TUR-byuh-luhnt)—In a state of disorder or chaos.

Index

African Diaspora   27
Afrika Bambaataa (Kevin Donovan)   14, 15
Asia   37, 40
back and forth   17
back spinning   16
back spins   21, 23
Battle of the Year (BOTY)   37, 38-39
battles   8, 23, 32, 33, 35, 37, 38-39, 41
b-boying   8-10, 13-14, 20-26, 33, 34, 35, 36, 37
Billboard   11
Black Spades   14
Boogaloo Sam (Sam Solomon)   23
break beats   8-9, 14, 16
break dancing (see b-boying)
Breakin' Convention   37
Bronx   7-10, 11, 12, 13-14, 15, 35, 37
Brooklyn   21
Cabbage Patch   27
Cali Swag District   29
call and response   17
Campbell, Don   26
careers   41
Checker, Chubby   33
choreography   16, 27, 33, 34, 37, 41
classes   5, 19, 41, 42
Combs, Sean (P. Diddy, Puff Daddy)   30
commercialization   21, 28-34, 37
Crazy Legs (Richard Colon)   35
crews   22, 32, 33, 37
cypher   23, 37
disco   11
DJ (disc jockey)   6, 7-18, 33
Doug E. Fresh   29
Dougie   28, 29, 31
downrocking   20, 21
Edwards, Braylon   29, 31
Electric Boogie (see West Coast funk: popping)
Europe   15, 35, 37, 38-39
fashion   18, 19
freestyling   22, 33-34
freeze   21
Funky Chicken   26
Furious Five   16-17
gangs   14-15, 17, 23
G.L.O.B.E.   22-23
"Good Times"   11
graffiti   14, 17-18, 35
Grandmaster Flash (Joseph Saddler)   12, 15-16, 17
Grand Wizard Theodore   16
griot   17
Harlem   11
Harlem Shake   30, 31
head spins   21, 24

Herculords   8
Hip-Hop Won't Stop: The Beats, The Rhymes, The Life   6
history of hip-hop   6-18, 20-26
Kool Herc (Clive Campbell)   6, 7-10, 12, 14
Manhattan   28
Martinez, Hugo   18
MC (master of ceremonies)   13-14, 16-17, 18
merry-go-round   8-9
movies   33, 35, 41
   Beat Street   33, 35
   Breakin'   33
   Krush Groove   33
   Style Wars   35
   Wild Style   33, 35
MTV   33, 37
Nomadic Massive   37
Philadelphia   17
Port-au-Prince, Haiti   37
power moves   21-23
Pow Wow   22-23
rap   11, 17, 18, 22, 29, 33, 35
"Rapper's Delight"   11
Rock Steady Crew   35
Roger Rabbit   26
Running Man   26, 27
scratching   16
six-step   21
Snake   27
So! What Happens Now?   35
Sugarhill Gang   11
Sunny Coast Skate   31
tags   17
television   32, 33, 37, 41
   America's Best Dance Crew   32, 33
   I Want to Work for Diddy   33
   T.I. and Tiny: The Family Hustle   33
toprocking   20, 21
turntabling   8-9
Twist   33
uprocking   21, 22
VH1   33
video games   33, 41
   B-Boy   33
   The Hip-Hop Dance Experience   33
Walk It Out   31, 33
Wall, John   28, 29
West Coast funk   23, 25
   locking   23, 25, 26
   popping (Electric Boogie)   23, 25, 26
windmill   19, 21
YouTube   29, 31, 42
Zulu Kings   14-15

About the Author

Marylou Morano Kjelle is a college English professor, freelance writer, and photojournalist who lives and works in Central New Jersey. Marylou has written dozens of books for young readers of all ages. She holds MS and MA degrees from Rutgers University, where she also teaches children's writing. When not teaching or writing, Marylou gardens, cooks, and bakes for her family and friends, watches movies, and reads as many books as she possibly can. Marylou enjoyed observing college students preparing for hip-hop dance competitions as she worked on this book.